A SAFE PLACE

Danny Priest

BookLeaf
Publishing

India | USA | UK

Presentation by BookLeaf Publishing

Web: www.bookleafpub.com

E-mail: info@bookleafpub.com

ISBN: 9789358361247

First edition 2021

DEDICATION

For the reader. May you find true comfort and security, wherever you may find it your safe place.

Thank you to Nathan and Sel for your incredible art and your unwavering friendship.

And for Elora, I am home now, thank you

1. EULOGY TO MY HAPPY PLACE

A eulogy to my happy place, or perhaps, a short list of fruit that will make you feel thirsty and completely miss the reason I am speaking; or, the story of me telling a complete stranger where the lighter is kept in my home. Whatever you decided to call it, let me start here. My safe place smells like mangoes, peaches, and passion fruit, a cacophony of tropical fruits that protect me for as long as I can keep inhaling. The scented candle sits idly on my desk. Still, cold, and lifeless, not unlike the one who watches it. The candle has not been lit for several weeks now, because the lighter is kept downstairs. Downstairs in the kitchen, in the drawer by the sink, I think, but there are people down there who I know deep down I should call Mum and Dad, but that never felt right to me, so for now, the lighter remains hidden away, like me. I know that if I go down there, the raging flames trapped inside that plastic prison will not wait until I am back upstairs to the safety of my bedroom, they will not wait for me to reach my sanctuary; no, it will be radiating heat from the moment I stray to retrieve it. It will scaled my flesh as I creep down the stairs, searing at my thin skin armour as I approach the kitchen, my heart now exposed... My wick. Ready to be whittled down a little more, and a little more, and a little more, and a lot more if it is a special occasion because we have family coming over and you want everything to be perfect, and a little more and a little more. Just another candle losing it's colour, losing it's scent, like so many before. I didn't go to my great grandmother's funeral, nor did I attend my grandma's funeral. I didn't go to my aunt's funeral because I was too busy wondering what song might be played at my funeral. My family don't know what my favourite songs are, or what my favourite flowers are, or that when they insult me, they are insulting nothing more than a carcass. A walking corpse that begs for the smell of mangoes, peaches and passion fruit, and longs for the warmth of a candle. My candle. My candle is burning, or, my candle is not burning because

I don't want to destroy it's self-esteem, making it feel like any less that it is, or, candles are burning for me, on a slab of concrete just ten feet away from where I would cower away from the world. Or maybe, I can blow out my own candle. I can make it my choice.

2. TAKEN

To take your love would be an honour and yet not the way in which I wish to possess it. Do I take it for my own by force, or perhaps with persuasion? Threatening or reasoning? Do I take it willingly, or otherwise? I wish to take it all the same. A drug of which there is an unlimited supply so slightly out of reach. An unexplainable high I yearn to intoxicate my mind with, to blur a world around me until it sits straight. Yet, if my thoughts were hazed, would I be able to take? Take in the beautiful view of your smile and hold the memory to me. I could stand atop this mountain, taking the sight deep inside me and it would still not be enough. One take was all it took to lose myself in you. You took your chance and now my heart is taken on an adventure unlike any other. A lowly pawn zooming across the board, feeling he could take on any other piece. No other could stand in my way for my love is taken, occupied. I would take a bullet for you while taking notes on how to be stronger, better for you. I would have my take of your world and ask no more than I deserve. Without you I am losing the best part of me, two take one is not one, you were my light and guidance. Without you I don't know which road to take or whether I can find the strength to the cross this chess board any longer. The queen is on the other side, protecting a different king, I take a final breath, and then another, taking in the world around me one more time, taking hold of the memories I have stolen and realise… I have taken only one thing, and I took it for granted. I don't know where I took it from, but I know, I have to return it.

3. GUIDING LIGHT

A wondrous nova hovers faintly in the distance. Such a distance... and yet, in a plane of absolute darkness, so hopeful. The empty fog and black sunlight that once flooded my reality has begun to flicker. "How did you find me out here?" I struggle to ask, as the enchanting wisp warms me from the inside out. My insides, radiant with her light. Hovering before my eyes, I see her, and I know I have been saved. Do you even know it; that you have rescued me from the abyss? One step forward, followed by another, and another, as I clumsily chase you into the eternal night. Eventually, the darkness around me begins to fade, my saving grace... I shout out to thank you. I scream my gratitude with empty lungs, my solar-powered voice has long since died. With everything with me, I find a lone whisper.

"Do you hear me? I love you." Further you fly, climbing and climbing out of the void, and across the ocean. This world is the one I want. Your luminescence glides across the still water below and reflects your beauty in every direction. Dazzling shards of silver glass echo from the pool beneath you. Out of nowhere, you surprised me. You stopped moving, stopped climbing away, stopped running from me. I have been given a chance to catch up to you, and now, before you, I am safe. No... more than that. I am not alone. I am not alone.

4.   DEATH'S BROTHER

Have you ever met with Death? Or perhaps his brother, Sleep?

When you close your eyes, under midnight skies,

He will visit you and weep. "Careful now little one, remember to awaken"

He warns us "before my brother comes and you soul has been forsaken."

Every breath we make each night, each noise we make, every turn,

Is another sigh from within his heart, and one less moment of concern.

He whispers to us now that the sun is rising. "Well done my child, for you have lived, and from the last day comes another.

But I know one day it will be your last, and you will greet my brother.

Goodnight Darling."

5. BELONGING

I take my home with me. Following roads, soaring skies, and crossing oceans, with me, always, is my home. The place where I belong is by your side, with a world in front of us. With everywhere to go and nowhere to be.

6. WINNING

I have been first before. The winning moments fleet like the dusty sun on a winter day, and before you have the chance to savour the sweet nectar of victory, you are back to being where you were before, being mediocre. There are always other people who will be faster, stronger, better looking, richer, more intelligent, more dignified, more polite, more, more, more than you are, so it comes down to this. Don't spend your life trying to be first. You don't have to be the funniest person she ever met. You don't have to be the most handsome, or most beautiful person they ever laid their eyes upon. You don't need money, nor do you need to impress her with your vast knowledge. I have been first before. Let me tell you, I would sooner be last. Let me be her last everything.

7.   THE LAST DAY OF EARTH

I had awoken, just in time to see the twilight glow of evening. That was the last time the sun ever set, for it never found the strength to rise again.

The streets were filled with cold, the flowers had all but withered.

There is no energy in the world, animals and plants alike turn to dust one by one.

Yet here I am standing at the end of it all, watching, already dead inside.

I am the only survivor

And I don't even feel like living.

8. LET THEM GO

Smile so the kings may seek you,

Do not grieve, they'll turn and go.

They will take you for your love and smiles,

But have no use for your woe.

Bear a child, one to replace them,

Watch them teeth and watch them grow,

Raise them to feel merry and high,

so they may leave us in the low.

Now, as one more passes,

Another body in the snow.

Now they beg for my forgiveness,

I vow to grieve, so you may go.

9. A LETTER FROM THE BOTTLE TO YOUR LIPS

Honey you're home! Welcome back sweetheart. You must be so exhausted after your long journey, taking your son to school, and then having to drive the whole way home, come in, come in. Relax. I'm right here, waiting for you. I'm waiting here with open… wow… Look at you, so… so… tired. Please allow me to kiss you, to revitalise you. Yes, yes, oh wow the taste of your dry, salty lips against mine is so refreshing. Your unbrushed breath in my mouth is so fulfilling, listen. The noise of the world around you drowns out, like your tongue in an ocean of pure crimson. I can see your body replenishing; colour returning to your cheeks, your tired eyes widening and then closing again, this is where you belong, with me, here. I can't understand how blind your family can be; how stupid your husband can be. Ignoring your beauty, forgetting your radiance. Why does he try to keep up apart? You know he knows about us. He asks you to stay away, but you can't. There is nobody that can separate us, our love is too strong, our bond is unbroken. Every time our lips say goodbye, I know it is merely a "see you soon". I know you will always come back to me, and I will wait for you. Patiently. In the dark. The cold. Wherever you decide to put me down, however long you leave, you know I will be here for you, you know I will love you unconditionally and you know, you know… that the colour is fading from your cheeks again. You know that you are slowing down, that you are eating less. My love for you stays strong, even if your lips now taste of stomach acid, and your tongue is stained a rotting golden shade. Your eyes fill with hollow sadness. By now, I know you well enough to be able to tell what you are thinking. You wonder whether those who loved you before will still love you now. Will they love you like I do?

10. TOMORROW

I am holding out

Hoping that tomorrow

I can forgive myself

For the things

I failed to do today

For tomorrow,

I am sorry.

11. EPHEMERALITY

Midnights come to pass.

Yearnings for the person who just wasn't right.

Sorrow for the moments already lost.

Mornings lost to the setting sun. Ice that clings to the heart and home.

Laughs once given so recklessly.

Even you, every you, and all the pieces of me you took with you.

12. PLAYTIME

When I was young, I found out that I could turn anything into a toy. Litter pickers, cassette tapes, pens, and even the vacuum, much to my mum's dismay. I suppose there is something powerful about a child's imagination that has the magic to bring something so mundane to life. A quality that can bring colour to even the dullest of objects. Toys became a thing of convenience. A void filler. I feared growing up, worried that one day I would be too old to play anymore. Too mature to be able to find a plaything in a pillowcase. It wasn't until I met you that I realised that this ability doesn't just disappear when you reach a certain age. You... You... You had the power to take something that was not fit for purpose and turned me into a toy. I became an object for you to pick up and fidget with as you pleased. Left in your bed when you were done with me, trapped in your room with your suffocating breath, guiding me, teaching me how to play with unfamiliar toys. You took my power away from me and the magic was lost. No longer could I turn pens and tapes into toys, or pretend that bath towels were magic carpets, I was presented with an object I could not figure out. A toy with no instructions. How did you manage to find enjoyment? How did you turn me into a toy?

13. LET ME TIDY THIS BEFORE I GO

Today I stopped loving the things that I love.

Collectives I have gathered for years are now thrown away.

The organised mess on my desk is now just a desk.

My space is just a space with no purpose like me.

But don't worry, you can just redecorate when I am gone.

14. LEARNING

Today I learned a truth,

One I wish to share with thee.

A feeling we all have known,

Is wishing we could be,

Someplace else, at work or home,

Can you begin to see?

I do not wish to be elsewhere,

Just somewhere away from me.

15. ON MY HANDS

Scalding water pours relentlessly at the flesh. The agony is unbearable, but the filth is worse. The disgusting dirt, mess that clings still to my hands, grasping between my fingers and hiding under my nails. Thick, like a grimy cage sown into my skin. Hot steam has filled my lungs but I still scrub. I scrub until my raw hands finally stretch open, the skin gives way and away melts the repulsive muck into the pool below. It flows, quite beautifully, down the drain. Slowly, but drifting constantly without lurching, as time always does.

16. ORGANISATION

A feeling that I could never begin to describe.

It was not death, for I am still standing.

The dead lay down. It was not comfort for my skin was quivering,

And the hairs on my arm stood to attention,

Loyal soldiers never sure where the next fight may come from.

If it were happiness I would be smiling,

'And when was the last time that happened?' I ask.

Well, it is also not cowardice, the scared would run.

Am I running? No. I am exploring this new feeling.

Is it hope? Not at all, who is there to put my faith into?

If not hope then, despair? Yes, that feels right.

No longer do I have to stand; I can finally lay down.

17. THE DRIVE

Flashing of the lamp posts, tapping of the rain,

Each another mile behind us, not to be seen again.

We watch the night pass by us, just like each road sign

With the moon always following, as the stars align.

Why do we keep on driving, if not to explore?

But instead to leave behind the fears we knew before.

A fear of the road catching us, as time itself will do,

For the gun outlives the holster, as the soul does me and you.

For now, we keep on driving, to escape the rising sun,

You and I alive forever, and forever on the run.

18. UNTITLED (I)

There is a future version of myself.

He is radiant, glowing and full of colour.

He waits patiently for me, open arms,

ready to comfort me, and remind me that,

I made it. I know he waits for me, grateful that I am allowing him
the chance to exist.

"You're welcome"

19. UNTITLED (II)

My name is a butterfly,

trying it's best to be beautiful, for you.

It dances around your lips carefully.

Your name reaches out to hold me.

The amber wing snaps in your names' grasp.